I Survived the System

Written by the survivors

The voices that were never heard

Honeybee Books

Published by Honeybee Books, Dorset
www.honeybeebooks.co.uk

Printed in the UK using paper from sustainable sources

ISBN: 978-1-913675-58-5

An Introduction

Hello, my name is Riley Gifford, and I am the primary editor and creator of this book.

Throughout my teenage years, and into early adulthood, I suffered immensely with my mental health, which sadly lead to numerous detentions under various sections of the Mental Health Act, including court of protection.

Not only did the system fail to protect me during these year's and treat my already rapidly declining mental health but heavily contributed towards a diagnosis of Complex PTSD (complex post-traumatic stress disorder).

Whilst in my first psychiatric unit at 15, I was diagnosed Autistic. It was after this I was told that being in here was the worst thing for me and it would make me more ill, yet I proceeded to be detained in this unit for 15 months, before being transferred to a more secure unit nearly 250 miles from home.

Instead of 'treatment', I received trauma, severe trust issues, a fear of anyone and anything medical, and little hope for a future.

Unfortunately, I am not an isolated case.

This is what lead me to creating this book, a collection of poetry and art created by survivors of the mental health system.

Our voices will not be silenced anymore.

Credit and thanks

I would say a huge thank you to all the authors who contributed to this book.

Without you all, this would not have been possible.

And a thank you to you, the readers, from us all, for purchasing and taking the time to read our work.

Profits made from sales are going to MIND, the mental health charity, with the hopes of raising awareness, aiding support, and who knows, maybe help change the system, so future generations don't have to suffer like we did.

To the Mental Health System:

Hospitals are supposed to be a place of safety, not somewhere that causes harm. Unwell children are supposed to be cared for and helped, not punished. Mental illness is an illness, not a choice.

We were not 'selfish', 'dangerous', 'too complex' or any of the other labels thrown our way.

We were poorly children, and you let us down.

Shame on you.

Contents

For us, the survivors.

In memory of our family and friends,

and the thousands of others who we lost.

The Truth

Behind the doors and behind my eyes I lie.
I lie and I wait, and I pray for change
because I cannot go back there again.
Everywhere I turn, I see it replay;
I feel the tears streaming down my face.
I want them to get off, I want them to let go, but no.

One turns to six, and now they're holding my wrists,
as the curtains are pulled and the blue gloves appear,
I know what's coming, but there is no running,
and I wish that someone could hear.
My cries for help, my fear-filled screams,
and then I remember they can, but no one is to be seen.
I can hear them all passing by, walking straight past
my door, while all along I'm pinned to the floor.
Hours pass, and the days turn to nights.
The darkness creeps in and steals all the light —
the light from the sky, the light from my eyes. Goodbye.

But still in the morning, I wake to the same,
the same stupid pain and the same messed-up brain.
Why?
I see people laughing like this is a joke,
and I wonder how, because when I try, I choke on the smoke. The
air gets stolen from my lungs and is replaced by toxins,
and I cannot see one.
One way to escape the pillow under my face.
My arms stretched above my head
as I'm held face down on the hospital bed.
This must be a dream, well, a nightmare I mean,
for these things should not be happening.

But you need to know, people need to be told,
what is shown on social media is not how it goes.

TikTok will show you patients dancing on the ward, but having a
tube forced down your nose is nothing to strive for.
TikTok will tell you hospitals are fun,
but I am not joking when I tell you the trauma cannot be undone.

It's not a 'grippy socks vacation' and this is not an allegation,
but do not believe when you cannot see the foundations.
The truth is painful, but the truth is true,
even though the truth I wish I never knew.
It needs to be spoken, and people made aware,
please, this isn't to scare, I am only telling you because I care.

My scars may seemingly fade,
though they will never fully be erased,
but if I can prevent the same wounds from appearing on you,
then you, I will try to save.

Riley Gifford

Trapped

In hectic halls where the bright lights hum,
A child sits still while the hours won't come.
The walls wear colours meant to soothe,
But nothing soft can smooth this bruise.
The bruise of waiting. The bruise of when.
The bruise of "you're not like them."
Outside, they grow, they run, and climb,
While I press pause on borrowed time.

The chairs are bolted.
The clocks run slow...
They say it's safe. They say it's 'right'.
But their hands grip tight in the hollow night,
And sometimes, when I try to fight,
The needle comes - And I take flight.
A burn, a sting, a bitter sleep—
The kind of quiet you don't want to keep.

But I feel buried inside my dream.
I watch them pass—those children free,
With scraped-up knees and untamed glee.
I am the echo they leave behind.
I am the page they didn't sign.
And though they tell me that time's my friend,
It feels like I am chasing a never-ending end.

So I sit in this place where the locked doors close,
Where loneliness blooms like a wilting rose.
Where days are counted in "individual needs"

And life is stitched where the old thread bleeds.
Perhaps one day I'll catch the sun.
Perhaps I'll heal. Or perhaps I'll run.
But for now, I drift where the buzzing hums.

Lyra Schmid

A Day in the Life

Wake up and line up, like a school kid, to take my meds.
As if a few pills could quiet the noise in my head,
As if the antidepressants would stop me from wishing I were dead,
As if my heart didn't feel like it's weighed down like lead.
I sit patiently waiting to go outside to a small garden
with fences too high to climb.
Fences made of metal bars, like mental illnesses,
are some kind of crime.
20 minutes max, then back inside.
Sat on a ward with no windows and no daylight,
I don't even know what the weather is like.
And that's where I stay till, I reach breaking point,
till I can't take the noise
Of that psychotic lady who talks to herself,
the one who screams as if she's in hell.
I don't blame her cause I want to too.
She might be confused, but half of what she says is true.
I take myself to a side room or my bedspace,
somewhere that's supposed to be safe,
Or I put on my headphones, and I pace.
In the corridor, up and down and up and down,
all the while my thoughts spin round, and round.
Staff regularly pass me by, but no one stops to ask if I'm alright.
So, I'll go and have a nap,
I sleep to avoid feeling like crap,
because sleeping is the closest thing to not existing.
To be honest, I don't think I would miss it,
being alive but trapped in my mind,
in a hospital miles and miles from home.
Then it's time for lunch, and there's another lady,
who can't eat on her own, another person deemed crazy, or lazy.

I wish I could help her because she's just so sweet,
but who am I in reality?
I'm not a staff member, that I've learnt,
and I can't help anyone when I can't help myself.
I'm better at giving advice than taking it,
and that's why I've fallen into this pit,
this state of not living, just barely surviving.
I'll read that quote about living and thriving,
and then I'll sleep some more to pass the time.
Just being here makes me tired.
Sometimes I'll have a little cry, but if anyone asks,
don't worry, I'm fine.
It reaches 8 pm, and that's when I take some more meds,
and then again, it's time for bed.
And that's how it goes, day in, day out.
If only to be heard, you didn't have to shout,
maybe, just maybe, I'd get support and go home,
And maybe, just maybe, I wouldn't feel so alone.

Rianna Lee

Nobody Sees

I'm not a person.
I'm a problem.
Something to manage, correct, and contain.
Just behaviours to fix,
Boxes to tick.
They don't care.
They don't listen.
They just control.
I don't get to decide,
And I'm forced to obey.
But if I fail,
I'm to blame.
Fear is defiance.
Silence, non-compliance.
Don't fight.
Don't question.
Just swallow the pill.
No means nothing.
It doesn't make it stop.
Not the pain, the panic, the shouting, the screams,
Not the force or the violence.
Nobody sees.
They've stolen my freedom.
They've stolen my voice.
They've taken things I didn't know could be taken,
Who I am -
No longer my choice.
My words have no weight.
They mean nothing, that's clear.
Not that it matters,
When there's no one to hear.

Because no one is coming.
No one even sees it as wrong.
Because I'm mistaken.
Irrational.
Delusional.
Wrong.
For power speaks,
And power wins,
And if you're not in control
You don't get believed.
So, what's the point of fighting?
I give up.
Head down.
Eyes closed.
Mouth shut.

Anonymous

Ticehurst

Ticehurst, Ticehurst, Ticehurst
I'm surprised that I didn't leave in a hearse,
Sometimes there wasn't even a single
'Permanent' nurse.
All you did to me was medicate, abuse
and restrain me,
I couldn't even be on my own to have a wee,
I would dream of running away from the
torture to be free.
They would restrain 15-year-old me naked,
My whole body felt degraded,
Then they would wonder why my self-harm escalated.

Kira Packer

Stars

Stars.
Something I never thought I would miss.
Stars.
Locked away with nothing but this.
Looking up and seeing nothing more than white ceilings,
Months on end, trying to escape my own wretched feelings.
Restrained like an animal and shown no grace,
Treated like nothing and caged in this forsaken place.
Attempting to heal, but each day traumatised,
'We are trying to help you' feels like nothing but lies.
The things I saw and the people I lost,
Being imprisoned like that to this day has a cost
Confined like I am nothing stays with me to this day,
This trauma I carry, it will never go away
You do not miss the water until the well runs dry,
And freedoms are the same, not missed until things go awry
But one silver lining amongst all the grief,
I will always appreciate and keep this belief
Being free is a blessing that no one should ever be denied,
The choice to be able to see the stars above and the beautiful blue sky
This freedom that was once taken from me,
But now I am better, I am happy and thank God I am free.
And the stars, the stars I can finally see.

Honor Burton

Humanity

I am not human.
in the physical body, of course, I am, but mentally
I lost sense of my humanity a while ago.
1,294 days to be precise.
the first time I was stripped of my rights
to freedom, dignity and privacy.
'You are now detained under section 2 of the Mental Health Act.'
Those words will forever echo in my head,
the phrase I've heard a dozen times now,
and the sentence I never want to hear again.
I was so innocent.
So innocent before hearing those words,
So innocent before admission,
number one of nine to inpatient units.
So innocent before experiencing three years
of trauma, abuse and neglect at the hands of 'professionals'.

Kiera Pye

Authorised Harm

They called it
care,
five men,
blue gloves, blank faces,
pinned me down,
injected silence into me.
I watched myself disappear
beneath muscle and protocol,
beneath the voice I wasn't allowed to have,
and tried to dissociate from the body,
that was no longer mine,
that had begun to flinch at the sound of keys.
And when they found out
about my childhood,
they laughed,
said I was lucky it wasn't them.
Said they'd do it
again
worse
if I didn't start 'behaving'.
Don't tell me it was care.
It was violence
dressed in a name badge,
sterile and systematic.
I remember the birds
outside my window
and the yearning to slip into their wing.
I remember what it cost to survive,
a body littered in bruises,
the constant terror,
The promise I would never leave.

Yet here I am,
free in body,
Rebuilding my mind.
And I will never call that
care.

Emily

`It's All For Him'

Same scars, same person.
He walked through hell,
so we could run today
and say the things
we were scared
to say.

Ross Cullen

Chipped and Frayed

I used to stare down at my hands filled with shells from the beach.
Their beauty and perfect imperfections amazed me;
some were shiny, some were worn.
Each one, a treasure that I would keep,
I always went back to find more.
Gripped them tight like a leech.
Now I take pity on the shells, I have become one too,
nothing to offer, nothing within my reach.
It's not pretty, sad and alone.
It's not fun being cold to the bone.
Brittle and fraying, chipped, decaying teeth.
Sound echoes through the void.
I used to think it was the ocean making that noise.
It's the hum of a slowing beat and whispers of those beginning to feel annoyed.
It's the crack of your neck and stumbling over chipped feet.
The whaling and screams are not the waves nor the wind;
it's the shrieking of the monsters' serenade.
I used to look at shells and take them home,
put them on a shelf, giving them a home.
Now I look at shells and hope that they can hear me.
How I hope that they can see another year.
That the sting in their chest gives it a rest,
and the shake in their legs can eventually head to bed.
The growing pit in their stomach no longer filled with dread.
And they don't have dreams of their mother finding them dead.
I hope the saltwater comes and washes away their tears
because someday soon, no one will be around
to turn the volume down on their silly little fears.

Jasmine Richard

The Complications of Being `Complex'

They handed me the prescription
said 'Don't worry, don't fret, these will numb your symptoms
We think it'll calm parts of your brain
It's part of your path to wellness; there's so much to gain
You may feel numb, you'll sleep, probably too much,
but if you're knocked out, you can't complain
Of course, there are side effects too, did we mention weight gain?
See, your condition for our service causes a lot of strain
So just agree, be quiet, take 3 of these a day
don't panic - antipsychotic is just a name
If you just comply, it's much better this way.'

So, I followed the doctor's order
tiny orange pill morning, lunch and evening
washed down with water
I say that as if there were much choice,
But when you're sectioned, there's little meaning to your voice.
See, this treatment programme was never without hesitation
But they promised there's a benefit from the sedation
So, the months continued, and I felt a change
This unfamiliar sense of slight stability building felt awfully strange
Because how do you know if you feel normal when, for years,
you're depicted as "deranged"?

I began to do things I had never got to do,
like time with friends, laughing -
less time spent in the emergency room
But still I stayed apprehensive,
My behaviours stayed at times destructive,
Medication has a place,
but therapy alongside would be constructive.

Seven years in the psychiatric system,
at least a year locked in a ward
But no effective therapy or psychological work had been explored.

Antipsychotic meds are great for sleeping 18 hours a day,
for causing hunger and appetite you didn't think could even be explained,
But Dr. reassures, 'just keep taking your meds
because it keeps your problematic behaviours restrained.
We're just going to ignore the reason you turned out this way,
Therapy would make you unstable,
and we don't have funding to contain your pain.'

So, in an all too familiar episode of distress that I couldn't withstand,
I found myself with my entire prescription in my hand.
And in no way was this new, but I didn't have it planned
a failed attempt at suicide, which shattered all progress firsthand.

Like every decision I made, or should I say I make, it was impulsive,
a choice I regretted the moment it happened,
Yet, to the powers that be, without any hesitation,
the overdose proved the pills were defective.
So, they took away my medication,
no reflection on the decision, nor hesitation
The doctors claimed that it was a clear demonstration,
twisting my moment of crisis into a claim of indication.

That prescribed chemicals weren't necessary anymore,
That the destruction and chaos I displayed was my ethos,
something deep in my core.
Perhaps untreatable, probably just the way I was born
I don't think there's a word that could ever depict,
to have a taste of stability given

and then suddenly ripped,
Would it be melodramatic to say I was grief-stricken?

Suddenly, symptoms I'd forgotten crept back into my mind,
imagine relief from your worst fears for months,
to have them all come back combined.
I needed my brain silent, and I knew who, where and why

And most know how the story tends to go
Just this one time, I can keep this under control
fucking hell, I would say it's just one pill, one line
Would you relax, I know what I'm doing,
it's fine but then suddenly it's not,
You promised yourself it's only short-term and you'd stop
at a certain time or a date, one day soon or whatnot
but it has a funny way of working once you're dependent,
addiction is well skilled at convincing you it's not present.
Even when it becomes apparent
that you can't even reach an hour without consuming a substance

And now doctors look at you with resentment and concern
The fact that you're unwell is still something they confirm

"But you take substances that we don't approve of,
you don't want our help; this is clear proof"

"Sure, if you got clean, we could try again
Although we don't have the resources to organise
any help to get you there
You did put yourself in this position to be fair"

How can a person's well-being and treatment be decided
by somebody who talks to you for an hour every few months -

Apparently, this is seen as frequent.
Just because they can read notes and have a degree
Somehow, this means they know what having my brain
and my day-to-day life is for me.
So, they refused my request for the treatment, they said originally
Although those were what I had been told
were needed to begin recovery
But of course, now I'm a walking drug dependency

Everything has changed
What once was a treatable symptom
supposedly cannot be explained
"We just can't tell what's caused by the drugs
or the defect in your brain
So, unfortunately, I will not be re-prescribing today"

It seems the general consensus is,
'K got herself into this mess; it's her job to end it'
It simply isn't our remit to treat dependency on substances
But if that goes away, we can reassess.
But what do you do when the very people
who are meant to be equipped for your issue,
decide that the support they provided previously
was going to be discontinued.
When the service built for your problem
drops you for getting worse,
when it feels like everybody is putting bets
on the arrival of your hearse,
when you've screamed out for help in countless different words
and now what for your average Joe would be an emergency
a suicide attempt - I mean, if carried out by me, holds no urgency
Services seem to have decided I fuck it up purposely.

So, if the day came that they missed all the signs,
on that day, I succeeded in my mission to die
I'm sure they'd palm it off as death by misadventure
a complete disregard for the help that I had begged for.

The system is fucked in every way, shape, and form
Yet the people in power choose to ignore
But how many more people must die
Before action is taken to prevent loss of life.

If I were you, I wouldn't hold your breath,
You'll be holding it until you reach death
And I'm sure the ambulance waiting time
It's too long to ensure you're revived.

Kira Gould

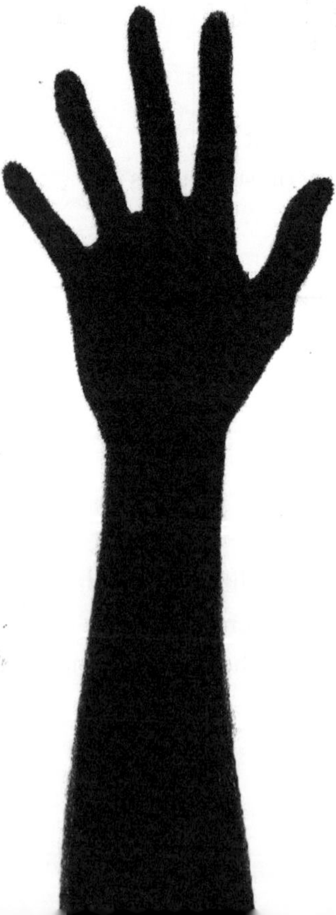

Shredded Soul

I think that
There will always be
A shred of my soul
Locked between
Those walls
At night
It cries out to me
Haunting my dreams
Begging to be freed
To come home
In my dreams
Those walls
Look different
But they have
The same feeling
Of that little
Tendril
Of hell
In my dreams
I am with that
Shred of soul
Desperately scraping
At those walls
Until my nails are torn
And my knuckles bloody
In my dreams
I am still that frightened
Little girl
Locked away
Forgotten by the world
No matter how much

Freedom I
Now have
No matter how far
I still run
My little shred of soul
Will still call out to me
Begging to
Be freed
From a place
That now only
Exists
In my dreams

Emily De Vine

Hello, Goodbye

One thousand goodbyes.
You would think I would be used to this by now,
but it cuts deep every time.
These will be the
most sore, leave the biggest wounds,
I won't lie.
More petty and shallow hellos all around,
Cannot be drowned.
Once again, I am going to shove
my life into boxes,
Stare blankly at a new ceiling and hold
Some paper as I cry.
Another floor where I will be kneeling.
This will take some healing.

Jasmine Richard

Will I Ever be Free?

I was a child when I first saw those lilac walls,
Those colours meant to calm,
Now activate my fight or flight,
Less care than harm.
I struggle to remember it clearly,
They ruined my mind with shocks,
Around 26 times, I think,
A tampered lock on Pandora's box.
Although the memories are mostly fragments,
I feel the rough seclusion gowns on my skin,
The dirty floors under my feet, the sheer despair,
There is no way to win.
No calming words or hope,
Just the cold, hard floor,
Finger-shaped bruises of varying ages,
So quick to put me down.
Echoes of cries and alarms down the corridors,
In my mind, I relive it all,
Echoes of laughter from the office
They took part of me and kept her.
How long will she still be in there?
That 16-year-old girl disguised as a crazed animal,
Held down on that floor by ghosts,
I want to let her up, set her free.
Sometimes I think I need to go back,
To help the souls still stuck there,
To let them know there's life beyond those lilac walls.
To let myself come home.

Yasmin Strain

Sorta, Kinda?

There's a house on the estate whose burglar alarm sounds exactly
like the one the staff would sound
And it's also broken, so it goes off maybe twice a month for hours.
Every time I wonder who's in trouble, and what trouble,
and if they'll be at dinner
And if so if they'll look different, bandaged or bruised
or bleeding from their head.

When I stuck stickers to my windows,
I had to throw out the butterflies
because they were identical to theirs,
the ones on the doors at the far ends,
the checkpoints for hours spent pacing
because what else was there to do?
And I feel like I'd never be able to sit still
if I had them on my windows
I feel like I'd always feel the need to walk up and touch them,
then move on to the next, et cetera,

I still eat hummus on toast for 30-40% of my meals,
it never hits right, the hummus is wrong,
and I've looked online to buy it in the tubs they had
But I've had no luck, so I settle for Lacklustre hummus on toast
and pretend it's the same.
It's still good, so I guess that's something I gained out of it all, but
I think I'd have eventually figured that out myself.

I forget about it most of the time until I get my blood taken,
and I see that flicker of their eyes to my arms.
It's usually followed by a slight widening,
then they relax as they see how old they are.

The oldest is over a decade now,
and even the youngest would be able to walk now
if they were human.
I can remember maybe 50% of their origins,
and of those 50%, 60% came after inpatient.

That's a pretty bad reflection of its success, I think.
A fear of alarms and butterfly stickers, a love for hummus and an
uncomfortable interaction every three months.
Also, nightmares, and the inability
for my family to look me in the eye sometimes.
No English language GCSE because the day I was taking it,
the staff scolded me for eating too much toast,
and that was all I could think about.

A million learnt new techniques for dying
that I have to pretend I don't know,
A box of letters and a painting of a sloth.
The number of calories in an apple is written on my eyelids.
A working knowledge of the streets of Bridgewater,
which will probably come in handy
if my train ever breaks down there,
but not a single other time.
Sort of funny stories I can tell,
so long as I omit the bad parts that would kill the vibe.

So, when I see a new counsellor now,
and they ask if I think I gained anything from it, I say
"Sorta, kinda?"

Rhiannah Tart

Hospital

The system broke me,
See the shit they did to me,
They injected me,
They said means things to me,
They laughed at me.
It still haunts me,
What they did to me,
They humiliated me,
They embarrassed me,
They left bruises on me.
Why didn't they help me?
Why did they hurt me?
They didn't care about me,
They abused me,
They traumatised me.

Kira Packer

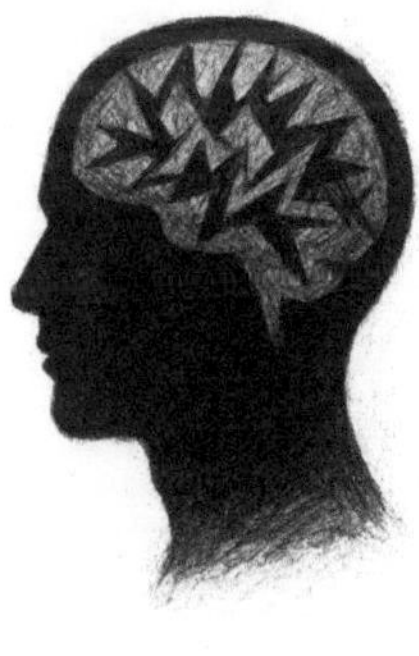

We Won't be Silent

Kayleigh Mason

Trust is Like Paper

Trust is like paper, but you know that.
You knew that when you listened to me explain how I find it incredibly hard to trust people,
yet you proved to me that I am right not to trust,
as you built up my hope just to tear me right back down.
And then you watched as I hit the ground.
Trust is like paper, but you know that.

You knew that when you told me that you wanted to hear my voice,
to then not only completely dismiss my words
but to make me believe they don't matter.
You knew that when you continuously made empty promises,
then watched, 'surprised' as I plummeted, and let me shatter.
And you knew that when you didn't think twice about
how your actions would affect me, like you hadn't seen it before,
then once again are frustrated when I don't want to put trust
in you and your 'We want what's best for you,' claim.

Trust is like paper, but you know that.
You've known that since the first time you ripped my paper,
yet you then proceeded to repeat the actions that caused so much
pain, and added another barrier, another layer.
You let this happen more times than I'd like to remember,
but to you, I am just a case number,
Right? I'm Insignificant.
You try to stick some tape on a tear and tell me,
'It'll be different this time'
But it is never different.

Trust is like paper, but you know that.
And it hurts more knowing you know that

because that really does mean you just don't care?
And I've never wanted to believe this,
I've tried to listen when others tell me
"It's not that they don't care, they're underfunded and understaffed,
the NHS are just so stretched"
But how long can this keep being the excuse you feed us?

Trust is like paper, but you know that
So please stop ripping the paper.
I put my trust in you too many times;
now I don't have any paper for you to rip anymore
And I don't know if I'm glad about that, or not…

Riley Gifford

Too Young

'You clearly want to be in hospital.'
I was told time, and time and time again.
'You're going to keep going inpatient until you change.'
I was fourteen.
All I wanted was for it to end, to be a golden child, to feel enough.
I look back now, and I was a child.
My sister is now that age.
She's a baby.
I was told as a child that I would be like this forever.
14.
One of the worst ages of my life.
You. Want. To. Be. In. Hospital.
My first admission, which I barely remember, was 3 hours from home.
Only one girl from the same county as me,
I barely knew what a unit was.
I was too young,
In the eyes of that ward, and everyone around me.
I felt grown up. I felt mature. I felt like I was prepared.
I could handle it.
I could not.
I was a child.
'We cannot help you'
A phrase I've heard over and over, and over.
They were right.
I was too young.
Too young to be helped.
Too young to be seen,
Too young to be understood.

Keira Pye

Depressive Detention

Welcome to the psychiatric hospital, we are here you your benefit. We will take your freedom in exchange for the chance of winning sanity.

Smile, you're on camera for your safety, we will take your laces, spray deodorant and your phone. The outside world doesn't need to know what goes on within these four padded walls.

I am here to explain the terms and conditions of your detention. You are here on a 28-day section because two or more mental health professionals think you need to remain in hospital for treatment, as you are a risk to either yourself or others.

Tomorrow you will wake up in a strange bed with plastic sheets, no lock on your bathroom door and magnetic curtains, but it's okay because your safety is our number one priority!

Do remember to eat your meals, take your meds and attend groups to be in with a chance of leaving us early, although we want you to stay to receive the proper care you deserve, even if it's traumatic and leads to institutionalisation.

On a scale of 1 to 10, how likely are you to harm yourself? Don't worry, this 'confidential' and will only be shared with all health professionals and kept in your file, and it will determine if you remain here on an extended trial.

Ignore the alarms and the screaming, it's just the other service users and the meds refusers.

Restraint is always a 'last resort' when the thoughts in your head are left to distort.

When you leave, you will miss being here because plastic furniture and cutlery will become a comfort blanket and 24 hour surveillance a safety net. We do hope you don't come back but expect to see you soon as your mental well-being is under attack, and the system remains a revolving door. When the community team can't support we will admit you once more.

But don't get me wrong, it's not all that bad, some rare places help you truly heal through the sad.

Where there aren't enough beds, too short staff and enormous demand…

There is a mental health crisis and a compassionate care shortage that kills children and adults every year.

It's a weight too much to bear, but out there are nurses, consultants and support workers who try their best in a crumbling system, with crumbling walls; unfortunately, it's them who are left trying to carry it all…

Charley Hickman

Unkind Hands

Everybody hates parts of their body.
Wrong eye shape.
Too much skin.
Too much hair.
Not enough hair.
No straight teeth.
But when you've had unkind hands roam around your body,
Touching parts of you, you didn't want.
It hurts.
Months down the line, you think you're all better, but suddenly someone will brush over your arm or leg, and it feels like a burn reopening.
The slightest touch causes pain.
It feels physical, but it's not.
You can be lying on your side and roll over
and feel it all over again.
Like a wound reopening.
It hurts.
You begin to hate your body.
Always covering up like it's a crime to show skin.
Not feeling comfortable without baggy hoodies.
Pulling them down as far as they go to not show anything.
You feel so ashamed, even though it wasn't your fault.
You just hope that one day in time
you'll learn to love your body again.

Anonymous

Stardust

It was said I was Stardust, cracked in two
A mind like a moon with too many phases –
Not quite full, not quite new.
I wore my diagnosis like Saturn's rings:
Heavy, glittering, misunderstood.
I was sitting on a rocket-like, moon-bound chair
My particles all dissipated,
And turned to despair.
I was a nebula of need –
I whispered, 'Help me'
But my comment got lost.
Like a fleeting comet at speed,
Entering space wasn't quite what I expected
But I'll tell you the good
Before I move to a bad perspective.
Nurses and HCAs who stitched together
My sleepless nights
As the sun sank into the horizon,
Their eyes were lit with something so rare
A love for life,
That they wanted to share
Each patient to them was a messy constellation
That needed to be loved.
They'd hold your hand through every orbit –
Though they would be gloved,
There were times when
The sky looked unsettlingly dark
And with their voices, actions, and love
They would create a spark.
But there is a universe of bad
And discussions that need to be had

Why are delicate constellations like us
Being ripped apart at the seams?
Being told by consultants that
We'll never reach our dreams.
Why are we branded as earth-destroying meteorites?
When all we've known in our hospital life,
is alarms, disbelief and fights
Fights for freedom, fights for change
'Earth to mental health rocket, you seem
To have gone out of range'
Is that an admission that you don't want to hear us?
Because that is the point where we start giving in
We once shone so bright, now we are dim
Meds up to eyeballs, so we can no longer marvel at the stars
Who'd want to look at stars while we are stuck
Onwards, collecting scars.
I'll never forget the looks of disgust
The lack of beds, the lack of trust
And into the A&E disgust I was thrust.
Now I'm an astronaut of the Psych wards
Lost all hope and whatever glimmer I once had
Do you know the minimising label they give it?
'Oh, she's just sad.'
She's not a constellation, far less
She's an attention-seeking mess.

Grace Roy

I Remember

Sometimes, I can forget that I ever stepped foot in a hospital.

These moments are rare and fleeting.

I might be at a university social event, having drunk one too many cider-blacks, laughing with my friends who have no connection to my past life.

Or I might be at a concert, screaming along to Stick Season by Noah Kahan, cowboy boots and flannel shirt tied around my waist, stuck in a sea of people just as complicated as me.

These are the moments that keep me moving forward, reminding me I am more than what has happened to me.

You don't realise that you've forgotten until you remember again.

I'll slip away to the toilet, tipsy and stumbling down the stairs. I'll hastily pull my skirt down and sit, and in this quiet moment, I'll remember.

The thing about forgetting is that when you remember, it hits you even harder.

It's a very specific feeling, like getting a punch in the chest, air winded out of me, gasping for oxygen.

Then the pain travels down to my stomach as my brain flashes milliseconds of memories.

Hands. Screams. Tubes.

Blue beds. Blue meds. Blue gloves.

And I have no choice but to pull myself together, flush the toilet, breathe, unlock the door, and wash my hands.

Try to forget again. Drink more.

I'll go back to my friends; everything looks different now.

A grey pair of glasses lenses, making everything feel dull. Hazy. Dying.

I don't believe everything happens for a reason.

There is no reason why my teenage self, suffered in a state of fight or flight for five years, referred to only as my initials, receiving trauma instead of treatment.

I just want to forget those five years of my life, but I remember, and remember, and remember.

Mae Lewis

I've Lost Control

Riley Gifford

The Stranger Within

Visiting time.
I had waited a week to see her again.
Every day, filled with thoughts of her tormented thoughts,
Every hour, yearning, praying, pleading, loving from afar.
Every minute, missing her smile, her voice, her laughter!
Every second, her absence is a shadow, a longing, a physical pain.
Willing her to "Just eat," to come home.
All the time, believing her to be in the "right place" to heal.
Trusting.
Now, finally, it's nearly visiting time.
Ninety minutes to drive there.
Time to allow the stomach-churning anxiety:
How will it go this week? What will we talk about?
Should I talk of family life without her, of our plans that exclude her?
Will she even see me?
Should I ask her to please "Just eat," to come home?
All the time, believing her to be in the "right place" to heal.
Naïve.
It's time.
She enters the room, and there is no one but her.
Despite the staff and other families around us.
I smile brightly, falsely, pretending this is normal, pretending this is ok,
Looking for signs of my child within this shell.
But the stranger within my daughter offers little response.
Her eyes were dead and unfeeling; her body damaged, her mind broken.
She is a corpse, an imposter, lost.
Please, please, "Just eat." Come home.
All the time, believing her to be in the "right place" to heal.

Desperate.
The visit ends too soon.
Too soon and not quickly enough
For visiting this stranger in my daughter's body is agony,
I cannot breathe. I am stifled. I despair.
Yet she must not see this,
She has to know that I believe in her, I hold the hope for her, and she can do this!
She can "Just eat" to come home to us.
All the time, believing her to be in the "right place" to heal.
Fooled.
One day soon, but not soon enough,
those rose-tinted glasses will shatter across my face.
I will understand that the stranger within my daughter could not tell
Of the daily horror that surrounded her, consuming her.
I will understand that lies were told by reassuring, caring, gentle angels of mercy,
Who were never reassuring, caring and gentle towards my child,
But demons.
I will understand that in this place,
she could never "Just eat" to come home.
She was never in the "right place to heal", and I was….
Guilty.

Anonymous

What Was it Like°

You may have set me free,
But I will never truly be
Your grasp is now stronger than ever before
I'm looking to escape, but I see no door.
In my mind, it is a lot quieter now
But my heart still screams, silently somehow
I look around the same 4 walls as the day before,
Hoping to see something worth much more
than the demons jumping out of my mind,
A tap on the shoulder, I feel from behind.
A girl stands there, small yet so tall
Her eyes look like she's ready for the fall.
She greets me with her name,
Though in it she holds much shame
A smile crept from me
Unexpectedly, I feel somewhat happy
That is, until she starts pacing
Her mind is crumbling, body shaking
I remember where we are.
For a minute, I went far
Back to reality, the smile ripped from my face
Look at me, stuck in such disgrace.
She's just like me, too sad to ever be happy,
Too trapped to be free,
"Revolving door"
No, I am so much more.
Belittle me and let me down,
Some even tackle me to the ground.
Held against all my power,
People are watching me in the shower.
Dehumanised me every day,

No wonder I don't want to stay.
"We're only here to keep you safe…"
I left with more trauma and less faith
I lost friends under your care.
You should have been there...
Sorry?
Trust the people who left me be,
When I was hurting myself and those around me?
I won't.
I wish I could somehow heal and truly be,
free.

Kayleigh Zara

My Beautiful Daughter

She was born before her due date,
Even now, she hates being late.
She was a lovely, beautiful child
Very meek and mild
I fought to get her the help at school
But she didn't like looking like a fool
She often used to scream and shout
'Why am I always singled out?'
After an unhappy but successful time at school,
We upped sticks and moved to Cornwall.
Things were good for a while,
And all she seemed to do was smile
Though unfortunately, it wasn't long
Before things started to go so wrong
She started going out and coming back late
And her mood swings weren't great
I didn't know what was wrong,
My lovely girl seemed to be gone.
After a couple of years, and plenty more tears
My beautiful daughter was taken away.
I truly thought I had finally seen the day
When all the hard work would finally pay
That she would get the treatment she so desperately needed
But silly me, I was defeated.
Unfortunately, the treatment didn't come
And all the hard work was undone.
She was kept in hospital for over four years, and yes, there were loads more tears
She was moved to London with virtually no notice
I was distraught as it wasn't the closest
I couldn't visit as much as I wanted
All I felt was very daunted

After months of meetings, calls and texts
I wasn't sure what would happen next
I was absolutely delighted
When Rhian phoned me, very excited
She was moving to a hospital nearer to me
It was a brand-new unit right by the sea
Hopefully, she will recover
And I know one day she will forgive her mother
For trying to do what I thought was best
For years and years, I could not rest
So, if you have a story like mine
You must devote a lot of time
You need to do what you think is right
Then hopefully you will sleep at night.

Lynee Gentry

The Journey

Sophie Smith

Crisis

People call the crisis team,
The 'cri-shit' team for a reason...
They tell us to have a cup of tea,
To have a bath,
To go on a walk.
But this doesn't help 99% of the people.
They don't understand how much their words hurt.
When they tell us it's okay to kill ourselves
Then they act surprised when we do.
Each time someone is successful
nothing changes and no one accepts they've
done wrong.
Yes, they are underpaid and overworked,
But that is no excuse for their words.

Keira Packer

Hidden Pandemic

Unlike any other virus...
We don't have to wear a mask:
But we do
We don't have to social distance:
But we do
We don't have to self-isolate:
But we do
We may "feel" we lose our friends:
But we don't
People see you happy and smiling
But inside we feel crushed
No sun, wine, chocolate, film, holiday
will take this emotional pain away
It's hard...to be kind to yourself
It's hard...to laugh
It's hard...to love
Although you don't feel it right now
Your family love you
Your friends love you
God loves you

THIS PANDEMIC IS CALLED
"A BROKEN SPIRIT"

PSALM 51:17
A Heart broken and crushed
O God, you will not reject

Alex Baldry

Trapped and Alone

From internally empty,
To empty promises
Full of threats and warnings
The signs were there
You treated me like a dare
Young and abused
Yet you used and abused your power
Medicated to be kept tame
It wasn't to keep me safe
I wasn't safe
Locked away, rights taken
Said I was complex situation
Dehumanized
Victimized
Traumatized
Why would you make me feel more alone?
Suicidal and hopeless became lifeless
Wanted to die
But it was for attention, right?
'You are a lost cause'
'You are too complex'
'You are never going to get better'
'You aren't even trying'
Words shouted in a place of safety.
Where was my safety?

Maizy Cortez

Letters from the U18s psych unit.

Some part of me remains, there in antiseptic rooms with alarms on every wall and staff who pin me like a butterfly to a mounting block, a cocoon suspended from space and time to nurse what is broken back into a shape suited for the world outside. As such I can't speak for it, that self that died every night after lights out to be dragged back with every morning medication call. But somehow I have pieces of it, from scrawled letter entries set afloat like messages in bottles, drifting to me unknowingly.

9/5/2017

Ended up snapping my headphones because they were wrapped so tightly around my neck.

We would hold each other, keep one another safe from the self, for whilst it didn't care much for its own preservation, our world became the others. I still hold my strange companions back from easy to wipe walls, keep soft furnishings to soften the blows and wake to bloody rooms. Most times it felt as if the adults couldn't bear to touch us in our despair, as if it was contagious, other times it was as if they couldn't wait to dig their fingers in, to make us still.

10/5/2017

Still on line-of-sight and still going to be on observations for a while.

Something monstrous, I will read my paperwork from when I was something beastly to the HCAs and public, something to be kept away where it could wail and thrash until the PRNs were doled out, something to be prodded and marvelled at in the council required therapy.

11/5/2017

Still on line-of-sight and had to take more medication on top of my usual morning meds

Three years later and I will still be pinned down by adults three times my size, ignored as I screech my way trying to tear myself apart to be free in some way, the water inviting from where I am restrained and all seems possible if I just make it to just beyond the horizon.

Medication for the nation- circa 2019

There was more to it than this, but this is all that remains, that which has carved its place here in my present. It feels like a stranger I wish to avoid, we are forced to share a table at a party neither of us want to be at. I'm sure there's a metaphor somewhere there if only the room wasn't so loud and the music was less suffocating.

5/6/2017

"I just get really, really scared. I might not be allowed out tomorrow…"

Just like that I am 14 again, hiding from the staff down a linoleum corridor with my friends, playing cards fluttering around us as we cackle and spin singing some Amy Winehouse song, running through the unit in fluffy socks as we are never let out, never seen by visitors, never to exist truly other than in the brief moments we are lit from the inside out by some shared madness.

18/6/2017

I want to see stars, be outside at night. Just to stare at the immense velvet blue black studded with stars. Limbo is all there is in this psych ward, we are kept waiting, the date to our freedom keeps shifting back, the referral a pipe dream. At least our meds keep us sedate, waking just to move to the common room to sleep all together on the floor curled around one another. Better that than being awake, aware and scheming, plotting on our downfall with increasing desperation and for lack of a better word: resourcefulness.

4/8/2017

I am tired all the time. I would say I hate it, but it helps numb things out. However, it makes me sad that we are always half asleep even when with each other... I would like to sleep but it doesn't come naturally anymore.

Imposter, embarrassing really to have survived that excruciating angst and hate, to still be here no matter the sworn promises forged in blood baying for death and destruction.

?/8/2017

These are all shallow useless things I won't achieve. But if I did… maybe people would be scared so I won't need to deal with…things. It's stupid. Best solution is death.

And yet, the world didn't end when I was 13. Nor did it all those times when I was 14, 15, 16 or 19.

Not for lack of trying, I hasten to add. And yet it made its way outside, limping and scarred. It's still there.

Morgan Gibbs

Olde to Win

All I've ever wanted is to win,
Instead, I end up in a ward
Getting tips on how to scratch my skin
No shoelaces, no power cords
No handle on the bathroom
No feeling that I've ever, ever caused
Underpaid workers, mis treating every issue
As I see the girls burning everything they're
Walking towards,
I don't remember how I got here
But it's clear other people in the halls
Think like me,
Kept under boundaries of psychiatry.
Nurses get tired
The cut it grows wide
And the only bit of sympathy is only given
By the same people who walk the ward with me
Day turns to night.
Alarm after scream
Don't know if the youth is ever going to feel right
Got told I was a lost cause,
By the same people begging for their lunch break
their care it's all fake,
Just a paycheck for every kid who's lost
I just keep asking
Why, why, why, why.

Ross Cullen

The Mother's View

The truth is, I only got through it by desperately searching for one tiny positive each day, no matter how small, and clinging to it with everything I had. I couldn't carry the weight of it all - so I forced myself to leave each day behind.

Even now, years later, it's hard to look back. I haven't fully dealt with what we went through. The pain is still there, unspoken.

During that time, allegations and safeguarding concerns were raised against me, even though all I wanted was to protect her. I spoke out when things were wrong and tried to be her voice when she couldn't use her own.

I just wanted my little girl home.

She was the one kept there - but I suffered too.

Jennie Gifford

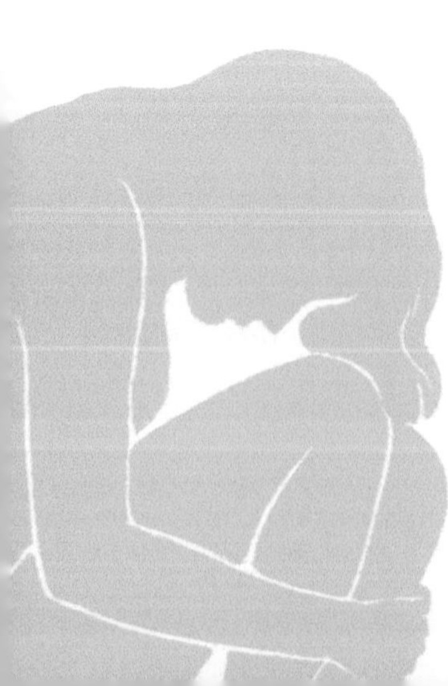

Different

My knee is not shaking subtly.
The first voice is rather quiet,
the second even more so.
A peculiar silence for the evening.
With the arrival of the day,
came a state of sanguineness.
A jive in my stride,
with an essence of confidence, pride.
A peculiar notion for the morning.
Ah ha a pattern, I see it now.
Classic Seamus has sunken in,
no stability for our Seamus.
The fallen have fell and the abyss rising.
Waiting, waiting, waiting...
for the second voice to fight.
To wade through the wonders of a madman.
Only silence remained, the second voice never came.
Untouched, everything remains.
The abyss is only six miles deep, you know...
Resilience remained.
I see now, why I don't see you,
you are not needed, for now.
I miss you, and maybe we'll meet again,
maybe not.
It'll be nice to see you again, it'll be nice if I don't.
But I thank you sincerely.

Keira J Delerue

Here to be Left

So here we are again, this dreaded point,
where you leave and send me on my way.
You know I don't feel ready but
you insist on departing.

The return to the open gate,
go through she softly says, I resist,
her hand slowly pulls away.

Fields of bracken - sharp reminders
of a past, dimly lit but not entirely dark.
not yet.

Stepping out, cautious and reserved,
A faint figure of Joan appears, reassuring,
Not entirely alone at least.

This help will live inside of you,
for there is more light further down the road.
May it be a banker's lamp, with a Persian rug
Hugging clapping the wooden piano nobile.

One will continue to manoeuvre.
One can indeed.

Shoulders down, spine spread straight,
A deep breath, lips sealed, curious eyes,
Remain curious comrade.

The help will live inside of you -
neatly packed, signed and secure.
Awaiting its next use, when required.

It hasn't died, it's just folded up,
Anticipating for the collapse and to be your side,
Holding on.

It is you, part of you now, at least.
Don't be a fool and think you've been abandoned,
although it may feel like that.

It has been said before, and it will be spoken again,
I see now, why I don't see you.
Look how far you have come,
Don't shade all that is behind.

Little strides and an inquisitive marvel of a mind.
Endure gentleness,
allow the aspects their empire,
demonstrate a clemency they were never shown
And you will be incandescent.

Refuse to be a rabble-rouser.
Faith is fickle but I compel this communion.
Trust is subsiding but you are out of harm's way,
sustained by your own structure and sanity,
We hope.

Keira J Delerue

A message to anyone who is currently battling the system

It might feel like you're fighting a losing battle but do not stop fighting for the correct treatment; the support you deserve. Never stop speaking up when things aren't right, keep shouting until someone listens, because someone will.

It might take a while, and an awful lot of shouting but do not give up.

If you are the loved one of a patient, I know you're exhausted - but keep showing up for them. They might push you away and say they hate you, but one day they will thank you for all that you're doing.

Always remember to look after yourself as well, and reach out if you're struggling.

This is hard for you too and you are just as important and worthy of support.

If you are a patient, you WILL make it out, do not listen to anyone who tells you otherwise.

There is hope for a life outside of all of this and things really can get better.

The system may be broken but you are not.

Never forget that.

BV - #0047 - 091025 - C0 - 203/127/4 - PB - 9781913675585 - Matt Lamination